THE 'WUNDERBAR' WORLD OF GERMAN IDIOMS

75 Everyday Idioms & Sayings with Translations & Example Sentences

Emma Jackman

emmalovesgerman.com

Front cover design:

'Where the fox and hare say goodnight to each other' (page 40)

Copyright © 2022 Emma Jackman

All rights reserved.

ISBN-13: 9798448252693

No part of this publication may be reproduced, distributed, or transmitted in any form or by any means, including photocopying, recording, or other electronic or mechanical methods, or by any information storage and retrieval system without the prior written permission of the publisher, except in the case of very brief quotations embodied in critical reviews and certain other non-commercial uses permitted by copyright law.

Table of Contents

Preface 1
Free Audio Download 2
Die Daumen drücken 3
Einen Kater haben 4
Ein Gehirn wie ein Sieb haben 5
Zwei Fliegen mit einer Klappe schlagen 6
Muskelkater haben 7
Auf dem Spiel stehen 8
Etwas steht vor der Tür 9
Wie ein Stein geschlafen 10
Die Nase voll haben / die Schnauze voll haben 11
Du spinnst! 12
Auf dem Holzweg sein 13
Im Eimer 14
Auf die Palme bringen 15
Aus einer Mücke einen Elefant machen 16
Das kommt mir Spanisch vor 17
Viel um die Ohren haben 18
Was zum Henker! 19
Den Faden verlieren 20
Unter vier Augen 21
Es hagelt Katzen 22
Den Buckel runterrutschen 23
Wie ein Elefant im Porzellanladen 24

Der Kern des Problems 25

In den sauren Apfel beißen 26

Schwein haben 27

Nicht der Rede wert 28

Wie ein begossener Pudel aussehen..29

Hals über Kopf..30

Über alle Berge sein...31

So ein Theater machen...32

Schnee von gestern 33

Übung macht den Meister..34

Es schüttet wie aus Eimern 35

Jemanden unter den Tisch trinken 36

Um den heißen Brei herumreden 37

Einen Stock im Hintern haben 38

Nur einen Katzensprung entfernt...39

Nur ein Steinwurf entfernt 39

Wo sich Fuchs und Hase gute Nacht sagen 40

Hunde die bellen beißen nicht..41

Brotlose Kunst sein...42

Den Kopf in Sand stecken..43

Schmetterlinge im Bauch haben 44

Auf den Keks gehen...45

Die Katze aus dem Sack lassen..46

Auf die Schliche kommen..47

Einem geschenkten Gaul schaut man nicht ins Maul 48

Die Katze im Sack kaufen..49

Ich bin fix und fertig 50

Das Ohr abkauen...51

Nicht die hellste Kerze auf der Torte 52
Mit halbem Ohr zuhören 53
Wenn die Katze aus dem Haus ist, tanzen die Mäuse 54
Das liegt auf der Hand 55
An der Nase herumführen 56
Hoch die Hände, Wochenende! 57
Auf den Arm nehmen 58
Durchdrehen 59
Mit den Hühnern aufstehen 60
Gesagt, getan 61
Da bin ich überfragt 62
Wie ein Pferd arbeiten 63
Ich verstehe nur Bahnhof 64
Der Hammer 65
Den Wald vor lauter Bäumen nicht mehr sehen 66
Hundewetter 67
Alles für die Katz 68
Das versteht sich von selbst 69
Mit Kanonen auf Spatzen schießen 70
Ein Brett vor dem Kopf haben 71
Eine Hand wäscht die andere 72
Es liegt mir auf der Zunge 73
Immer mit der Ruhe 74
Reden ist Silber, schweigen ist Gold 75
Auf den Leim gegangen 76
About the Author 78

Preface

Welcome to the Wunderbar World of German Idioms.

You probably use idioms every day in English, without even thinking about it. They enrich language and bring speech alive. Plus they are great fun to use and learn. Just like the English language, German also has a colourful collection of idioms for every possible situation.

Learning German idioms, *Redewendungen*, is a great way to improve the flow of a sentence and to get a meaning or feeling across that would otherwise be difficult to express. They will improve your fluency. You learn them as a 'chunk' which will give more thinking time for the rest of your sentence.

Because English is a Germanic language, you'll notice that we share some idioms, or have some which are very similar. Others will seem very different and it may be difficult to find an English equivalent.

Have fun learning some of these idioms and sayings and be sure to use them in conversation to really fix them into your head.

Free Audio Download

As a small token of thanks for buying this book, I'd like to offer a free bonus gift exclusive to my readers.

All the German idioms and example sentences are available as a free MP3 download, so you can hear the correct pronunciation as you read along in the book.

You can download the free audio here:

emmalovesgerman.com/free-audio

Die Daumen drücken

Literal Translation: To squeeze / press the thumbs

Meaning: To wish someone luck

English Equivalent: To cross your fingers

Example:

> Ich hoffe nur, dass es nicht zu spät ist, ich **drücke dir die Daumen**.
>
> I just hope it's not too late, I'll cross my fingers for you.

Example:

> **Drück mir die Daumen!**
>
> Cross your fingers for me!

Einen Kater haben

Literal Translation: To have a tom cat

Meaning: To have a hangover

English Equivalent: To have a hangover / to be hungover

Example:

> Was für ein Abend! Aber jetzt **habe ich einen Kater**.
>
> What an evening! But now I have a hangover.

Example:

> Er hat so viel Bier getrunken, dass er am nächsten Morgen **einen schrecklichen Kater hatte**.
>
> He drank so much beer, that the next morning he had a terrible hangover.

Ein Gehirn wie ein Sieb haben

Literal Translation: To have a brain like a sieve

Meaning: To be very forgetful

English Equivalent: To have a brain like a sieve

Example:

    Wie heißen Sie nochmal? **Ich habe ein Gehirn wie ein Sieb**.

    What are you called again? I have a brain like a sieve.

Zwei Fliegen mit einer Klappe schlagen

Literal Translation: To hit two flies with one swatter

Meaning: To get two things done at once

English Equivalent: To kill two birds with one stone

Example:

Ich gehe einkaufen und hole gleichzeitig meine Schwester ab. So **schlage ich zwei Fliegen mit einer Klappe**.

I'm going shopping and will pick up my sister at the same time. So I'll kill two birds with one stone.

Muskelkater haben

Literal Translation: To have muscle tom cat

Meaning: To have muscle pain after exercise

English Equivalent: To have pulled muscles

Example:

> Oh Mann! Gestern war ich im Fitnessstudio und jetzt **habe ich Muskelkater**.
>
> Oh man! Yesterday I was in the gym, and now I have pulled muscles.

Auf dem Spiel stehen

Literal Translation: To stand on the game

Meaning: To be in danger / at risk

English Equivalent: Something is on the line / at stake

Example:

>Ich habe so viele Fehler gemacht, jetzt mein Job **steht auf dem Spiel**.

>I've made so many mistakes, my job is on the line.

Etwas steht vor der Tür

Literal Translation: Something stands in front of the door

Meaning: Something is going to happen very soon

English Equivalent: Something is around the corner

Example:

    Endlich **steht der Frühling vor der Tür**.

Finally Spring is around the corner.

Wie ein Stein geschlafen

Literal Translation: To have slept like a stone

Meaning: To have had a very good night's sleep

English Equivalent: To sleep like a log / to sleep like a stone

Example:

   - Hast du gut geschlafen?
   - Ja, ich habe **wie ein Stein geschlafen**

   - Did you sleep well?
   - Yes, I slept like a log

Die Nase voll haben / die Schnauze voll haben

Literal Translation: To have the nose / snout full

Meaning: To have had enough of something / to be annoyed or irritated by something

English Equivalent: I've had it up to 'here'

Example:

    Ich **habe die Nase voll** von dir!

    I've had it up to 'here' with you!

Example:

    Ich **habe die Schnauze voll** von meinem Job!

    I've had it up to 'here' with my job!

Note: While the two phrases can be used interchangeably, *ich habe die Schnauze voll*, is used to express even more annoyance than *ich habe die Nase voll*.

Du spinnst!

Literal Translation: You spin!

Meaning: Used to say to someone 'you're mad' or 'you're crazy'

English Equivalent: You're mad

Example:

Du hast dein ganzes Geld für Lottoscheine ausgegeben? **Du spinnst!**

You spent all your money on lottery tickets? You're mad!

Auf dem Holzweg sein

Literal Translation: To be on the logging path

Meaning: To have got something wrong / misunderstood something

English Equivalent: To be barking up the wrong tree

Example:

Sie glauben, Sie hätten Recht, aber **Sie sind auf dem Holzweg!**

You believe you're right, but you're barking up the wrong tree!

Im Eimer

Literal Translation: In the bucket

Meaning: To be very tired / broken

English Equivalent: To be totally knackered

Example:

    Ich muss mein Auto in die Werkstatt bringen. Es ist **im Eimer!**

    I have to take my car to a workshop. It's broken!

Example:

    Ich habe so viel zu tun, ich bin **im Eimer!**

    I have so much to do, I'm knackered!

Auf die Palme bringen

Literal Translation: To bring someone on the palm tree

Meaning: To make someone very angry / to drive someone mad

English Equivalent: To drive someone up the wall

Example:

Das bringt mich auf die Palme!

It drives me up the wall!

Example:

Manchmal **bringt** mein Vorgesetzter **mich auf die Palme.**

Sometimes my manager drives me mad.

Aus einer Mücke einen Elefant machen

Literal Translation: To make an elephant out of a mosquito

Meaning: To make something seem worse than it actually is

English Equivalent: To blow something out of proportion / to make a mountain out of a molehill

Example:

> Ich habe einen kleinen Fehler gemacht, und er hat **aus einer Mücke einen Elefant gemacht**.
>
> I made a small mistake and he blew it out of proportion.

Das kommt mir Spanisch vor

Literal Translation: That seems Spanish to me

Meaning: To express lack of understanding

English Equivalent: It's all Greek to me

Example:

> - Hast du eine Ahnung, was er sagt?
> - Nein, **das kommt mir Spanisch vor**!
>
> - Do you have any idea what he's saying?
> - No, it's all Greek to me!

Viel um die Ohren haben

Literal Translation: To have a lot around the ears

Meaning: To have a lot to do / a lot going on

English Equivalent: Up to one's ears

Example:

    Ich **habe** zurzeit **viel um die Ohren**.

    At the moment I have a lot going on.

Was zum Henker!

Literal Translation: What the executioner!

Meaning: Used as an exclamation / in surprise

English Equivalent: What the heck!

Example:

    Was zum Henker ist hier los?

    What the heck is going on here?

Example:

    Was zum Henker habe ich gerade gesehen?

    What the heck did I just see?

Note: Be careful about where you use this phrase. If you treat it like the English equivalent and be mindful about who you say it to, you should be ok.

Den Faden verlieren

Literal Translation: To lose the thread

Meaning: Used when you forget what you were going to say / don't follow the conversation

English Equivalent: To lose your chain of thought

Example:

>Du hast mich unterbrochen, jetzt habe ich **den Faden verloren**.

>You interrupted me, now I've lost my chain of thought.

Example:

>Wenn viele Leute Deutsch sprechen, **verliere ich** manchmal **den Faden**.

>If a lot of people are speaking German, sometimes I lose the thread.

Unter vier Augen

Literal Translation: Under four eyes

Meaning: Wishing to speak to someone face to face, away from others

English Equivalent: In private / face to face

Example:

Ich würde lieber **unter vier Augen** mit meinem Manager sprechen.

I would rather speak to my manager face to face.

Example:

Es ist sehr persönlich, könnten wir **unter vier Augen** reden?

It is very personal, can we talk in private?

Es hagelt Katzen

Literal Translation: It's hailing cats

Meaning: It's raining very hard

English Equivalent: It's raining cats and dogs

Example:

> Ich gehe nicht nach draußen, **es hagelt Katzen**!
>
> I'm not going outside, it's raining cats and dogs!

Den Buckel runterrutschen

Literal Translation: Can slide down my back

Meaning: Used to tell someone to 'go away' or 'stop bothering me'

English Equivalent: Get lost! / Go sit on a tack!

Example:

>Ich habe dir schon mal gesagt, dass ich nicht interessiert bin!
>**Du kannst mir den Buckel runterrutschen!**
>
>I've told you already that I'm not interested! Get lost!

Wie ein Elefant im Porzellanladen

Literal Translation: Like an elephant in a china shop

Meaning: Used to describe someone who is very clumsy

English Equivalent: Like a bull in a china shop

Example:

>Ehrlich gesagt, er ist so ungeschickt. Er ist **wie ein Elefant im Porzellanladen**.

>To be honest, he's so clumsy. He's like a bull in a china shop.

Der Kern des Problems

Literal Translation: The core on the problem

Meaning: To indicate the main issue that is causing a problem

English Equivalent: The heart of the problem

Example:

Ich bin nicht mutig genug, Deutsch zu sprechen. **Das ist der Kern des Problems**.

I'm not brave enough to speak German. That's the heart of the problem.

In den sauren Apfel beißen

Literal Translation: To bite into the sour apple

Meaning: To describe the feeling of having to do something unpleasant

English Equivalent: To bite the bullet

Example:

> Du musst einfach **in den sauren Apfel beißen** und dich entschuldigen.
>
> You just have to bite the bullet and apologise.

Schwein haben

Literal Translation: To have pig

Meaning: To be lucky

English Equivalent: To have a stroke of luck

Example:

>Du hast **Schwein gehabt**!

>You got lucky!

Nicht der Rede wert

Literal Translation: Not worth the talk

Meaning: To express modesty, not wanting thanks for something

English Equivalent: Don't mention it / It was nothing

Example:

    - Ich danke dir für deine Hilfe.
    - **Nicht der Rede wert**.

    - Thank you for your help.
    - Don't mention it.

Wie ein begossener Pudel aussehen

Literal Translation: To look like a wet poodle

Meaning: Used to describe someone who is soaking wet

English Equivalent: To look like a drowned rat

Example:

    Regnet es? Du siehst aus wie ein begossener Pudel.

    Is it raining? You look like a drowned rat.

Hals über Kopf

Literal Translation:	Neck over head
Meaning:	To do something impulsive, without thinking. Also used to describe falling madly in love.
English Equivalent:	Headlong / On the spur of the moment / Head over heels (in love)

Example:

Sie hat nicht aufgepasst und ist **Hals über Kopf** gegen einen Baum gelaufen!

She wasn't paying attention and ran headlong into a tree!

Example:

Er verliebte sich **Hals über Kopf** in sie.

He fell head over heels in love with her.

Über alle Berge sein

Literal Translation: To be over the mountains

Meaning: To describe someone who has left in a hurry / without a trace

English Equivalent: (To run) for the hills / to be long gone

Example:

    Sobald sie von Heirat sprach, war er **über alle Berge**.

    As soon as she mentioned marriage, he ran for the hills.

Example:

    Der Bankräuber war schon **über alle Berge** mit dem Geld.

    The bank robber was already long gone with the money.

So ein Theater machen

Literal Translation: To make a theatre

Meaning: To describe someone making a fuss over nothing

English Equivalent: To kick up a fuss

Example:

Das Essen war kalt und deswegen hat er **so ein Theater gemacht**.

The food was cold and he kicked up a fuss because of it.

Example:

Mach nicht **so ein Theater**!

Don't make such a fuss!

Schnee von gestern

Literal Translation: Snow from yesterday

Meaning: To describe something that is no longer relevant

English Equivalent: Yesterday's news / water under the bridge

Example:

> Jan ich weiß, wir hatten unsere Probleme, aber das ist **Schnee von gestern**.
>
> Jan I know we had our problems, but that's water under the bridge.

Example:

> Ja ich bin über sie hinweg. Sie ist **Schnee von gestern**.
>
> Yes, I'm over her. She's yesterday's news.

Übung macht den Meister

Literal Translation: Practice makes the master

Meaning: If you practice / work on something you will master it

English Equivalent: Practice makes perfect

Example:

> Es stimmt, dass Deutsch schwierig ist, aber **Übung macht den Meister**.
>
> It's true that German is difficult, but practice makes perfect.

Es schüttet wie aus Eimern

Literal Translation: It's pouring like buckets

Meaning: To describe when it's raining very hard

English Equivalent: It's pouring / it's bucketing down

Example:

Ich gehe auf keinen Fall raus, **es schüttet wie aus Eimern**.

There's no way I'm going out, it's pouring down!

Jemanden unter den Tisch trinken

Literal Translation: To drink someone under the table

Meaning: To be able to drink more than someone else (a challenge)

English Equivalent: To drink someone under the table

Example:

Das klingt nach einer Herausforderung! Ich könnte dich leicht **unter den Tisch trinken**.

That sounds like a challenge! I could easily drink you under the table.

Um den heißen Brei herumreden

Literal Translation: To talk around the hot porridge

Meaning: To talk a lot without getting to the point

English Equivalent: To beat around the bush

Example:

>Frau Schmitt, ich will nicht **um den heißen Brei herumreden**.
>
>Mrs. Schmitt, I won't beat around the bush.

Einen Stock im Hintern haben

Literal Translation: To have a stick up the butt

Meaning: Used to describe someone who is very uptight / serious

English Equivalent: To have a stick up the butt

Example:

Meine neue Kollegin **hat** einen richtigen **Stock im Hintern**.

My new colleague has a right stick up her butt.

Nur einen Katzensprung entfernt

Literal Translation: Only a cat jump away

Meaning: To describe something that is very close by

English Equivalent: Only a stone's throw away

Example:

Der Strand ist **nur einen Katzensprung** vom Hotel **entfernt**.

The beach is only a stone's throw away from the hotel.

Nur ein Steinwurf entfernt

Literal Translation: Only a stone's throw away

Meaning: To describe something that is very close by

Usage: Used in the same way as *nur einen Katzensprung entfernt*.

Wo sich Fuchs und Hase gute Nacht sagen

Literal Translation: Where the fox and hare say goodnight to each other

Meaning: To describe a place that is very remote

English Equivalent: In the middle of nowhere / in the sticks

Example:

> Wir haben in einem kleinen Dorf Urlaub gemacht, **wo sich Fuchs und Hase gute Nacht sagen**.
>
> We had a holiday in a small village, in the middle of nowhere.

Example:

> Sie ist es leid, dort zu leben, **wo sich Fuchs und Hase gute Nacht sagen**.
>
> She is bored of living in the sticks.

Hunde die bellen beißen nicht

Literal Translation: Barking dogs don't bite

Meaning: When someone seems meaner than they actually are

English Equivalent: Someone's bark is worse than their bite

Example:

> Hans **bellt nur, er beißt nicht**.

> Hans bark is worse than his bite

Example:

> Anne ist wie ein **bellender Hund, sie beißt nicht**.

> Anne's bark is worse than her bite.

Brotlose Kunst sein

Literal Translation: To be a breadless art

Meaning: To be unprofitable

English Equivalent: There's no money in it

Example:

Ich fange an zu glauben, dass Musiker zu sein, eine **brotlose Kunst ist**.

I'm beginning to think that there's no money in being a musician.

Den Kopf in Sand stecken

Literal Translation: To stick the head in the sand

Meaning: To ignore what is going on around you

English Equivalent: To put your head in the sand

Example:

>Er hat so viel Geldsorgen, aber er **steckt einfach den Kopf in den Sand**.

>He has so many money worries, but just puts his head in the sand.

Schmetterlinge im Bauch haben

Literal Translation: Butterflies in the stomach

Meaning: To be nervous

English Equivalent: To have butterflies in the stomach

Example:

Vor dem ersten Date **hatte ich Schmetterlinge im Bauch**.

Before the first date I had butterflies in my stomach.

Auf den Keks gehen

Literal Translation:	To get on the cookies

Meaning:	To be annoying

English Equivalent:	To get on one's nerves

Example:

> Der Typ **geht mir auf den Keks**.
>
> That guy is getting on my nerves.

Example:

> Das schlechte Wetter **geht mir auf den Keks**.
>
> The bad weather is getting on my nerves.

Die Katze aus dem Sack lassen

Literal Translation: To let the cat out of the sack

Meaning: To accidently say something that was otherwise secret

English Equivalent: To let the cat out of the bag / to spill the beans

Example:

> Eigentlich sollte es eine Überraschungsparty werden, aber Martin hat **die Katze aus dem Sack gelassen**.
>
> Actually it was supposed to be a surprise party, but Martin let the cat out of the bag.

Auf die Schliche kommen

Literal Translation: To come on the tricks

Meaning: To find out about something

English Equivalent: To get wise to someone / to catch on

Example:

> Dachtest du, ich würde nicht **auf die Schliche kommen**?
>
> Did you think I wouldn't catch on?

Example:

> Er hoffte nur, dass der Chef ihm nicht **auf die Schliche kommen** würde.
>
> He just hoped that the boss wouldn't get wise to it.

Einem geschenkten Gaul schaut man nicht ins Maul

Literal Translation: One doesn't look a gifted horse in the mouth

Meaning: Don't be ungrateful for a gift

English Equivalent: Don't look a gift horse in the mouth

Example:

> Es war ein sehr großzügiges Geschenk. **Einem geschenkten Gaul schaut man nicht ins Maul**.
>
> It was a very generous gift. You shouldn't look a gift horse in the mouth.

Die Katze im Sack kaufen

Literal Translation: To buy the cat in the sack

Meaning: To buy something blind / without seeing it

English Equivalent: A pig in a poke / to buy blind

Example:

>Wenn du das Auto nicht Probe fährst, **kaufst du die Katze im Sack**.

>If you buy the car without test driving it, you're buying blind.

Ich bin fix und fertig

Meaning: To be very tired

English Equivalent: To be knackered / pooped

Example:

    Ich habe bis 3 Uhr gefeiert und jetzt **bin ich fix und fertig**.

    I was partying until 3am and now I'm totally pooped.

Das Ohr abkauen

Literal Translation: To chew someone's ear

Meaning: To talk so much the other person doesn't get a chance to speak

English Equivalent: To chew someone's ear off / to talk the hind legs off a donkey

Example:

Es tut mir leid, dass ich dir den ganzen Morgen **das Ohr abgekaut** habe.

I'm sorry for chewing your ear off all morning.

Example:

Ehrlich gesagt, meine Freundin hört nicht auf zu reden. Sie **kaut mir das Ohr ab**!

To be honest, my girlfriend doesn't stop talking. She can talk the hind legs off a donkey!

Nicht die hellste Kerze auf der Torte

Literal Translation: Not the brightest candle on the cake

Meaning: To describe someone who is not very intelligent

English Equivalent: Not the sharpest tool in the shed

Example:

Er ist ein netter Typ, aber **nicht die hellste Kerze auf der Torte**.

He is a nice guy, but not the sharpest tool in the shed.

Mit halbem Ohr zuhören

Literal Translation: To listen with half an ear

Meaning: Not listening to someone properly

English Equivalent: To be half listening

Example:

Du wirst kein Deutsch lernen, wenn du nur **mit halbem Ohr zuhörst**.

You don't learn German if you're only half listening.

Wenn die Katze aus dem Haus ist, tanzen die Mäuse

Literal Translation: When the cat is out of the house, the mice dance

Meaning: When someone of authority isn't around, everyone can relax and have fun

English Equivalent: When the cat's away, the mice will play

Example:

Meine Eltern sind dieses Wochenende weg, und ihr wisst: **wenn die Katze aus dem Haus ist, tanzen die Mäuse**.

My parents are away this weekend, and you guys know: when the cat's away the mice will play.

Das liegt auf der Hand

Literal Translation: It lies on the hand

Meaning: When something is very obvious

English Equivalent: It's obvious / duhh!

Example:

    - Gefällt dir dein Job als Schokoladekoster?
    - **Das liegt auf der Hand**!

    - Do you like your job as a chocolate taster?
    - Obviously!

An der Nase herumführen

Literal Translation: To lead by the nose

Meaning: To cause someone to spend more time on something than is necessary

English Equivalent: To string someone along

Example:

    Der Verbrecher **führt** die Polizei **an der Nase herum**.

    The criminal strings the police along.

Hoch die Hände, Wochenende!

Literal Translation: Hands high, weekend!

Meaning: Used as an exclamation to celebrate the arrival of the weekend

English Equivalent: TGIF! (Thank God it's Friday!)

Example:

    Was für eine Woche! **Hoch die Hände, Wochenende**!

    What a week! TGIF!

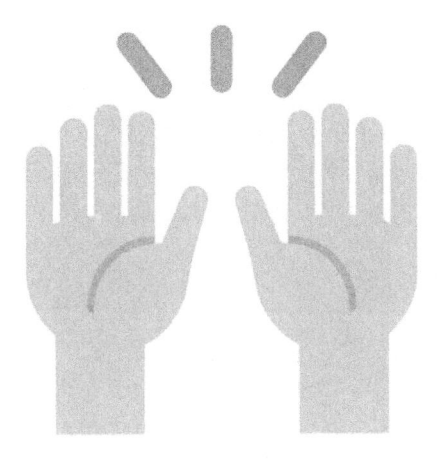

Auf den Arm nehmen

Literal Translation: To take someone on the arms

Meaning: To fool / trick someone

English Equivalent: To pull someone's leg / to wind someone up

Example:

    Willst du mich **auf den Arm nehmen**?

    Are you pulling my leg?

Example:

    Ich bin mir nicht sicher, ob er es ernst meint oder mich **auf den Arm nimmt**.

    I'm not sure if he's serious, or if he's winding me up.

Durchdrehen

Literal Translation: To spin

Meaning: Used to describe someone who has been pushed to the edge and has had enough

English Equivalent: To freak out / to lose it

Example:

Wenn mein Chef mich noch mehr unter Druck setzt **drehe ich durch**!

If my boss puts me under any more pressure I'll lose it!

Example:

Wenn deine Mutter davon erfährt wird sie **durchdrehen**.

If your mother finds out about this she'll freak out.

Mit den Hühnern aufstehen

Literal Translation: To get up with the chickens

Meaning: To get up very early

English Equivalent: To get up at the crack of dawn

Example:

>Jeden Morgen **steht sie mit den Hühnern auf**.

>Every morning she gets up at the crack of dawn.

Example:

>Mein Flug war so früh, dass ich **mit den Hühnern aufstehen** musste.

>My flight was so early that I had to get up at the crack of dawn.

Gesagt, getan

Literal Translation: Said, done

Meaning: To complete a task very quickly, almost before it's been started

English Equivalent: No sooner said than done

Example:

Gesagt, getan. Das Projekt wurde innerhalb einer Woche abgeschlossen.

No sooner said than done. The project was completed within a week.

Da bin ich überfragt

Literal Translation: There I am 'over asked'

Meaning: Used when you have no answer to a question

English Equivalent: Beats me!

Example:

    - Glaubst du, sie kommt zurück?
- **Da bin ich überfragt**!

    - Do you think she'll come back?
    - Beats me!

Wie ein Pferd arbeiten

Literal Translation: To work like a horse

Meaning: To work very hard

English Equivalent: To work like a dog

Example:

    Als ich jung war, **arbeitete** mein Vater **wie ein Pferd**.

    When I was young, my father worked like a dog.

Ich verstehe nur Bahnhof

Literal Translation: I only understand train station

Meaning: To not understand something / to be confused

English Equivalent: It's as clear as mud / it's all Greek to me

Example:

> Die Anweisungen machen keinen Sinn. **Ich verstehe nur Bahnhof**.
>
> The instructions don't make sense. I don't understand at all.

Example:

> Verstehst du Plattdeutsch? **Ich verstehe nur Bahnhof**!
>
> Do you understand low German? It's all Greek to me!

Der Hammer

Literal Translation: The hammer

Meaning: Used for something that's fantastic / awesome

Example:

    Das Konzert war **der Hammer**!

    The concert was awesome!

Den Wald vor lauter Bäumen nicht mehr sehen

Literal Translation: To not see the forest for the loud trees

Meaning: When you can't concentrate on something because there is so much going on / to feel overwhelmed

English Equivalent: You can't see the wood for the trees

Example:

Sie hat bei der Arbeit so viel zu tun und **sieht den Wald vor lauter Bäumen nicht**.

She has so much to do at work, and can't see the wood for the trees.

Hundewetter

Literal Translation: Dog weather

Meaning: Used to describe bad weather

English Equivalent: Filthy weather / lousy weather

Example:

    Wir haben hier in Norddeutschland heute **Hundewetter**.

    We have lousy weather here today in North Germany.

Alles für die Katz

Literal Translation: Everything for the cat

Meaning: To put a lot of effort into something, but it was a waste of time

English Equivalent: All for nothing

Example:

> Ich habe die ganze Woche an diesem Projekt gearbeitet und es war **alles für die Katz**.
>
> I worked on this project the whole week, and it was all for nothing.

Das versteht sich von selbst

Literal Translation: That's understood by itself

Meaning: When something is so obvious it doesn't need mentioning

English Equivalent: That goes without saying

Example:

    Natürlich werde ich hingehen, **das versteht sich von selbst**.

    Of course I'll go, that goes without saying.

Mit Kanonen auf Spatzen schießen

Literal Translation: To shoot sparrows with cannons

Meaning: To be heavy handed

English Equivalent: To use a sledgehammer to crack a nut

Example:

Ich glaube nicht, dass du dafür einen Hammer benutzen sollst. Das ist so, als würde man **mit Kanonen auf Spatzen schießen**.

I don't think you should use a hammer on that. It'd be like using a sledgehammer to crack a nut.

Ein Brett vor dem Kopf haben

Literal Translation: To have a board in front of your head

Meaning: To describe someone who is obtuse / a bit stupid

English Equivalent: A bit thick / dumb

Example:

> Ich habe versucht, es meinem Kollegen zu erklären aber er hat **ein Brett vor dem Kopf**.
>
> I have tried to explain it to my colleague, but he's a bit stupid.

Eine Hand wäscht die andere

Literal Translation: One hand washes the other

Meaning: To do a favour for someone and get a favour in return

English Equivalent: One good turn deserves another / you scratch my back, I'll scratch yours

Example:

>Sie haben mir wirklich geholfen und **eine Hand wäscht die andere**.

>You have really helped me, and one good turn deserves another.

Es liegt mir auf der Zunge

Literal Translation: It's on the tongue

Meaning: Used to express when you know a word / answer but can't quite remember it

English Equivalent: It's on the tip of my tongue

Example:

    Ich kenne dieses Wort, **es liegt mir auf der Zunge**!

    I know this word, it's on the tip of my tongue!

Immer mit der Ruhe

Literal Translation: Always with the peace / quiet

Meaning: Used to tell someone to calm down

English Equivalent: Take it easy

Example:

    Immer mit der Ruhe, wir verpassen den Bus nicht.

    Take it easy, we won't miss the bus.

Reden ist Silber, schweigen ist Gold

Literal Translation: Talking is silver, silence is gold

Meaning: Used to describe a feeling of relief when peace and quiet is restored

English Equivalent: Silence is golden

Example:

Endlich sind die lauten Leute weg! **Reden ist Silber, schweigen ist Gold**.

Finally those loud people have gone! Silence is golden.

Auf den Leim gegangen

Literal Translation: To have gone on the glue

Meaning: To fall for someone's trick / scam

English Equivalent: To be hoodwinked / to be hustled

Example:

Ich kann nicht glauben, dass sie diesem Online- Betrüger **auf den Leim gegangen** ist.

I can't believe she was hustled by that online scammer.

What did you think of this book?

First of all, thank you for purchasing 'The Wunderbar World of German Idioms'. I know you could have picked any number of books to read, but you picked this book and for that I am extremely grateful.

I hope that it helped you to understand more about German idioms. If you found this book helpful, it would be great if you could share this book with your friends and family by posting to Facebook and Twitter.

If you enjoyed this book and found some benefit in reading this, I'd like to hear from you and hope that you could take some time to post a review on Amazon:

amazon.com/review/create-review

Your feedback and support will help me to greatly improve my writing craft for future projects and make this book even better.

About the Author

Emma Jackman is the founder of EmmaLovesGerman.com. She started learning German as an adult at the age of 34 after many years of visiting Germany but being unable to speak the language.

She is dedicated to helping others learn to love the German language as much as she does, and to make this sometimes confusing language, that bit easier.

EmmaLovesGerman.com is an all-round resource for German learners. There you'll find articles about speaking, reading, listening and writing in German as well as simplifying German grammar, explaining frequently used phrases and reviewing online language courses and resources.

Other Books by This Author

Everyday German Phrases for Beginners

Are you at the beginning of your German learning journey? Maybe you're planning a trip to a German speaking country and want to make a good impression by trying out some simple German phrases.

Whether you're serious about studying German or just want a grab and go resource, in this book you'll discover over 400 easy German words and phrases which can be used in everyday situations.

Each chapter covers a certain phrase such as 'nice to meet you', 'how are you?', introductions, ordering food etc. and dives deep into all the different ways to say that phrase.

Available on Kindle & paperback on Amazon

The Wunderbar World of German Idioms Vol. 2

Are you hungry for more German idioms?

Does learning German 'give you a neck'? It's true that there's a lot about the German language that's 'no sugar lick'. But when you have fun with it through German idioms, you'll sound more like a native speaker, improve your fluency and have a lot of fun along the way.

'The Wunderbar World of German Idioms Vol. 2' will take you on a journey to discover 75 more everyday German idioms and sayings, all approved by native German speakers.

Available on Kindle & paperback on Amazon

Printed in Great Britain
by Amazon